MEET THE PLANETS

By Yvette Mitchell

Library For All Ltd.

Meet the Planets

First published 2021

Published by Library For All Ltd
Email: info@libraryforall.org
URL: libraryforall.org

This book was made possible by the generous support of the Education Cooperation Program.

Meet the Planets
Mitchell, Yvette
ISBN: 978-1-922647-33-7
SKU01719

MEET THE PLANETS

I am Mercury.

I am Venus.

I am Earth.

I am Mars.

I am Jupiter.

I am Saturn.

I am Uranus.

I am Neptune.

We are the planets.

Photo Credits

You can use these questions to talk about this book with your family, friends and teachers.

What did you learn from this book?

Describe this book in one word. Funny? Scary? Colourful? Interesting?

How did this book make you feel when you finished reading it?

What was your favourite part of this book?

download our reader app
getlibraryforall.org

About the contributors

Library For All works with authors and illustrators from around the world to develop diverse, relevant, high quality stories for young readers. Visit libraryforall.org for the latest news on writers' workshop events, submission guidelines and other creative opportunities.

Did you enjoy this book?

We have hundreds more expertly curated original stories to choose from.

We work in partnership with authors, educators, cultural advisors, governments and NGOs to bring the joy of reading to children everywhere.

Did you know?

We create global impact in these fields by embracing the United Nations Sustainable Development Goals.

library for all.org

www.ingramcontent.com/pod-product-compliance
Lightning Source LLC
Chambersburg PA
CBHW040319050426
42452CB00018B/2920